Jonathan Holmes has worked for public broadcasters on three continents for over forty-five years. He joined the ABC as *Four Corners* executive producer in 1982 and retired in 2013 after five years of presenting *Media Watch*. Holmes still reports occasionally for ABC TV.

Writers in the *On Series*

Fleur Anderson
Gay Bilson
John Birmingham
Julian Burnside
Blanche d'Alpuget
Paul Daley
Robert Dessaix
Juliana Engberg
Sarah Ferguson
Nikki Gemmell
Stan Grant
Germaine Greer
Sarah Hanson-Young
Jonathan Holmes
Daisy Jeffrey
Susan Johnson
Malcolm Knox

Barrie Kosky
Sally McManus
David Malouf
Paula Matthewson
Katharine Murphy
Dorothy Porter
Leigh Sales
Mark Scott
Tory Shepherd
Tim Soutphommasane
David Speers
Natasha Stott Despoja
Anne Summers
Tony Wheeler
Ashleigh Wilson
Elisabeth Wynhausen

Jonathan Holmes
On Aunty

Every attempt has been made to locate the copyright holders for material quoted in this book. Any person or organisation that may have been overlooked or misattributed may contact the publisher.

hachette
AUSTRALIA

Published in Australia and New Zealand in 2020
by Hachette Australia
(an imprint of Hachette Australia Pty Limited)
Level 17, 207 Kent Street, Sydney NSW 2000
www.hachette.com.au

First published in 2019 by Melbourne University Publishing

10 9 8 7 6 5 4 3 2 1

Copyright © Jonathan Holmes 2019

This book is copyright. Apart from any fair dealing for the purposes of private study, research, criticism or review permitted under the *Copyright Act 1968*, no part may be stored or reproduced by any process without prior written permission. Enquiries should be made to the publisher.

A catalogue record for this book is available from the National Library of Australia

ISBN: 978 0 7336 4450 4 (paperback)

Original cover concept by Nada Backovic Design
Text design by Alice Graphics
Author photograph by Alex Barry
Typeset by Typeskill
Printed and bound in Australia by McPherson's Printing Group

The paper this book is printed on is certified against the Forest Stewardship Council® Standards. McPherson's Printing Group holds FSC® chain of custody certification SA-COC-005379. FSC® promotes environmentally responsible, socially beneficial and economically viable management of the world's forests.

The public interest

I worked for the ABC, off and on, for thirty years. For most of that time, I was a program-maker: an executive producer, a field producer, a reporter, and for five years the presenter of *Media Watch*. I spent a short time in the 1980s as a head of department, but I don't pretend to know much about senior management; and I retired from the ABC five years ago, so this is not—at least so far as recent events are concerned—an insider's story.

I am also seventy years old: only fractionally above the average age of those who watch broadcast television on the ABC's main channel. That is a frightening statistic. A decade ago it was around fifty-five.

A Senate committee is currently inquiring into alleged political interference in the ABC. In one sense, there is nothing new in this. The ABC has been browbeaten for most of its eighty-six years by politicians—especially, but by no means exclusively, conservative politicians, who tend to regard it as a hostile media organisation. Before he reached the top of the greasy pole, Malcolm Turnbull liked to portray himself as an exception: a conservative politician who understood and appreciated Aunty's role in the media landscape.

Yet during his time as prime minister the pressure on the ABC from the coalition he led—on its reporting, its budget, its governance—was unremitting and unprecedented. In June 2018, the national Liberal Party conference voted by a large majority to privatise the ABC. Not a single delegate spoke in opposition to the motion.

It didn't help, of course, that the ABC was chaired for much of that time by a man who apparently thought that the way to safeguard the Corporation's future was to 'get rid of' journalists who upset its paymaster, the government of the day.

But the ABC faces a far more serious problem today than political pressure: like most mainstream media organisations, it is in the throes of digital disruption. The threat, in the long term, may well be existential. Its commercial rivals have seen their revenues plunge, as audiences desert newspapers, television and radio for digital platforms owned by international behemoths that suck up the advertising revenue that used to go to them.

The ABC doesn't face that immediate threat. According to its latest surveys, 83 per cent of Australians believe it performs a valuable role. So long as it can sustain that kind of public support, the politicians will continue to fund it, at least to a degree. But Aunty's audiences, too, are deserting broadcast television and radio. It has been desperately trying to reconfigure its organisational structure, and its content too, to pursue Australian audiences on the platforms they want to use. It has been attempting to achieve a 'transformation'.

That requires investment, at a time when the ABC's budgets are being remorselessly cut. It requires excellent change management; but instead staff morale is low, structures are chaotic, directions confused, clear decisions scarce. Above all, it needs a board and management with a realistic and united vision. Instead, there has been leadership chaos at the very top.

And yet, from Australia's country towns to its national capital, the need for a reliable, trusted and imaginative media organisation that is responsive to and sustained by citizens, not consumers, is arguably as great as it has ever been.

On Aunty isn't an attempt to dig up more dirt on recent turmoil at the ABC. I don't pretend to have a road map for its survival in the digital age. But I have spent most of my career trying, as best I can, to tell true stories in an engaging way; in other words, to interest the Australian public, in the Australian public interest. That's a task that still desperately needs to be done. If the ABC can't find a way to do it, I don't know who else will.

The week that was

Aunty had never known a week like it.

On 24 September 2018, the ABC board sacked its managing director just half-way through her five-year term. Many of the Corporation's four-hundred staff were delighted, or at least relieved. But Michelle Guthrie declared herself 'devastated'. She was not going to go willingly, or quietly.

Her return fire proved devastating.

On the Wednesday morning, we learned from Fairfax Media that the chair of the ABC, Justin Milne, had urged Guthrie to sack the ABC's chief economics correspondent, Emma Alberici, to appease the government. 'They fricken hate her,' he had emailed the previous May. 'I think it's simple. Get rid of her.'

By 1 p.m., the cavernous atrium of the ABC's headquarters in the Sydney suburb of Ultimo was crowded with hundreds of protesting ABC staff members. There were stop-work meetings in Melbourne and Brisbane too. Prophetically, as it would turn out, senior business reporter Stephen Long told the Ultimo meeting: 'Our board of directors needs to protect us from political interference from Canberra, not be a conduit for it.'

Almost every pundit and media outlet in the country—even the ABC's most implacable enemy, News Corp columnist Andrew Bolt—were by now calling for Milne's head.

But Milne said he was staying, and the board supported him.

So Guthrie launched a second torpedo. On the Thursday morning, Sydney's *Daily Telegraph* ran a double-page exclusive. In June, it reported, Milne had met with his friend and former colleague Malcolm Turnbull and Minister for Communications Mitch Fifield. Again, the politicians were wrathful—this time about the work of ABC News' political editor Andrew Probyn. In a phone call that day, reported the *Telegraph*, Milne had passed on that rage to Michelle Guthrie. Once again his solution was simple: 'You have to shoot him!' Milne had shouted. (Justin Milne, we learned later, completely rejects this version of the conversation.)

That morning at 11 a.m., Milne told *7.30*'s Leigh Sales that he had resigned to deflect the 'firestorm'. But he was unapologetic. His job was to secure the future of the ABC in the digital age. For that it needed money, and lots of it; and the government held the purse strings.

'You can't go around irritating the person who is going to give you funding again and again and again,' he told Sales, 'if it's over matters of accuracy and impartiality.'

Then came the most revealing exchange of all:

> SALES: Did you, as the chairman, breach a wall—breach your role, I guess—to be the wall between politicians wanting to influence the reporting of the ABC and the ABC's editorial independence?
>
> MILNE: No. Nobody has told me that I'm supposed to be a wall. I think, more what I'm likely to be is a conduit. You know, the Government is a fundamentally

important stakeholder in the ABC, and I think it's the role of the board to be a conduit so that the left hand knows what the right hand is doing and we understand how people are feeling about things.[1]

Not a wall, but a conduit: the very word that Stephen Long had used just the day before.

Mollifying people in power

It doesn't take a genius to recognise that public broadcasters funded by the taxpayer can all too easily be cowed into obedience by governments that hold the purse strings, unless their independence is fiercely defended.

If past chairs of the ABC have felt it necessary to pass on complaints they have received from government, most have done so discreetly. Never has a demand that a particular journalist be 'got rid of' to placate a government been committed to writing—or if it has, the indiscretion has been decently interred.

And yet, there are precedents. Those with the stamina to read Ken Inglis's monumental two-volume history of the ABC will come across episode after episode in which ministers and prime ministers—Labor as well as conservative—rail against what they see as Aunty's pernicious bias.

One famous example caused a media furore: Prime Minister Bob Hawke's public condemnation of ABC TV's coverage of the first Gulf War in January 1991. Its analysis, he told Sydney's *Daily Telegraph*, was 'loaded, biased and disgraceful'.[2]

I was one of the producers of the offending television program, a nightly one-hour special called *The Gulf Report*. The people working on the program were genuinely baffled by Hawke's outburst. It seemed to us, as I wrote just a few months after the war was over, 'that the totality of the coverage on the program had heavily favoured the war party as against the peace party, and the coalition view of the crisis as against Iraq's view—as indeed you would expect, given the overwhelming public support in Australia for the government's policy'.[3]

It turned out that Hawke's fury was directed primarily at one academic commentator whom we used heavily: Dr Robert Springborg, an internationally recognised expert on the politics of the Middle East. In earlier articles and media interviews—though not on *The Gulf Report*—Springborg had made clear that he opposed Israel's occupation of the West Bank and Gaza, thus antagonising Israeli sympathisers such as Hawke. And months earlier, Springborg had questioned the way Hawke had decided, without parliamentary approval, to offer Royal Australian Navy ships to join President Bush's coalition in the Gulf.

Publicly, managing director David Hill defended the impartiality of the ABC's coverage. But behind the scenes, after a face-to-face meeting with Hawke, Hill ordered that Springborg should be removed from the program, or at least 'labelled' so that his opinions were made known to viewers.

The ABC's controller of television news, Peter Manning, resisted this utterly impractical proposition. More disturbingly, according to Manning, Hill wanted one of the program's presenters, Geraldine Doogue, removed. Hill denies he wanted any such thing. The impasse between the two continues to this day. But Geraldine Doogue certainly believes that

Peter Manning saved her reputation and perhaps even her job. A decade later, during the second Gulf War, the episode still shocked and angered her: 'As I saw it,' she wrote in 2003 for the *Griffith Review*, 'I was being offered as the "ritual sacrifice" to make a nasty problem disappear. It had little to do with the quality of my work, much more to do with mollifying people in power.'[4]

The parallel with what happened—or didn't happen—in 2018 is remarkably close. David Hill denies that Bob Hawke asked him, or that he ordered Peter Manning, to remove Geraldine Doogue. Justin Milne denies that Malcolm Turnbull asked him, or that he ordered Michelle Guthrie, to 'shoot' Andrew Probyn. What's certain is that the 'people in power' in 2018 demanded mollifying as much as, or more than, any government in the Corporation's history—including the decade when John Howard held sway.

Between 2013 and 2016, Malcolm Turnbull was Tony Abbott's communications minister. He encouraged the perception, particularly inside the ABC, that he was a friend in the enemy's camp. Abbott made no secret of his hostility to the ABC—or rather, of his belief that it was hostile to him, to his government and to Australian interests.

When the ABC joined with *Guardian Australia* to publish documents leaked by Edward Snowden revealing that Australia had eavesdropped on the Indonesian President's phone calls, and shortly afterwards published allegations that Australian Navy sailors had tortured asylum seekers by deliberately holding their hands on hot pipes, the prime minister said that 'it dismays Australians when the national broadcaster appears to take everyone's side but our own'.

Not quite 'the enemy of the (Australian) people'—but not far off either.

In June 2015, *Q&A* allowed Zaky Mallah—a man who ten years earlier had been acquitted of terrorism charges, though he had pled guilty to threatening ASIO officers—to join its studio audience and to question a minister about the government's counter-terrorism legislation. Outrage followed. Abbott again told the ABC to ask itself, 'Whose side are you on?' And he told his party room, 'We all know the program is a lefty lynch mob.'

Abbott's mentor John Howard was never so unguarded in his language. But the way in which Howard treated the ABC during his decade in power provided a model that Abbott followed to a T.

Before the 1996 election, the coalition promised to preserve the ABC's funding. Before the 2013 election, Tony Abbott did the same.

In its first budget, despite its pre-election pledge, the Howard government slashed the ABC's budget by 10 per cent. In its first budget, the Abbott government slashed it by 5 per cent.

In 1996, the Howard government announced a review of the ABC's role and functions to be conducted by businessman Bob Mansfield. In 2014, the Abbott government instituted an 'efficiency review' of the SBS and ABC by former Seven Media CFO Peter Lewis.

Lewis advised that the public broadcasters could accommodate the swingeing budget cuts that had already been imposed, without cutting programs or services to the public. Convenient.

During the life of the Howard government, directors were appointed to the ABC board whose chief qualification seemed to be their publicly expressed hostility to the Corporation: Victorian Liberal factional heavy Michael Kroger; conservative columnist for *The Australian* Janet Albrechtsen; anthropologist Ron Brunton; historian, contrarian and later editor of *Quadrant* Keith Windschuttle.

The Rudd and Gillard governments enacted amendments to the *Australian Broadcasting Corporation Act 1983* which made such blatantly political appointments harder:

a list of candidates for the ABC and SBS boards would be drawn up by a non-partisan nomination panel appointed by the supposedly non-political head of the public service, the Secretary of the Department of Prime Minister and Cabinet.

In July 2014, the Abbott government boldly overrode those niceties to stack the nomination panel with two highly partisan appointees: Janet Albrechtsen (who had left the ABC board three years earlier) and former Liberal communications minister Neil Brown, an indefatigable critic of the ABC, who believed it should be privatised forthwith. In theory, these appointments were made by the secretary of the prime minister's department, Ian Watt. In September 2018, long after she'd left the panel, Albrechtsen confirmed that she'd been asked to serve on it by Tony Abbott himself.[5]

Inside the ABC, there was a sigh of relief when Turnbull ousted Abbott. But the pressure didn't ease: it got worse. Although those who worked in his office, as well as Turnbull himself, deny it, it looks in retrospect like a three-year assault on the ABC: in his desperate—and ultimately futile—attempt to appease the right wing of his party, his belief in the value of an independent, well-funded public broadcaster was one among many convictions that Turnbull was willing to betray.

It started with Turnbull's replacement as minister for communications: Victorian senator Mitch Fifield, an enthusiastic member of the Institute for Public Affairs, which has long advocated the abolition or privatisation of the ABC.

In March 2017, Turnbull appointed his friend and former OzEmail colleague Justin Milne to chair the ABC. He was on the list submitted by the nomination panel. But he told the Senate inquiry last November that he was encouraged to put his hat into the ring by Mitch Fifield directly.[6]

The minister, not the PM, is responsible for recommending to the governor-general all non-executive directors of the ABC and SBS. Since September 2015 Senator Fifield has appointed five non-executive board members. Only one, the current acting chair Kirstin Ferguson, was interviewed and recommended by the nomination panel. Two—Western Australian mining executive Vanessa Guthrie and Victorian investment banker Joseph Gersh—were interviewed by the panel, but not recommended. Two others—Queensland farmer Georgie Somerset and South Australian personnel expert Donny Walford—were not even considered by the panel.

The result is a board with plenty of experience in corporate boardrooms, but almost none in media management, let alone public broadcasting. Only one board member, other than staff-elected director Jane Connors, has significant experience in a media company— former Seven Media CFO Peter Lewis.

Like the Abbott government before it, the Turnbull government treated the nomination process set up by the Rudd and Gillard governments with contempt.

In June 2018, the federal Liberal Party's annual council voted by a two-thirds majority to privatise the ABC—with the enthusiastic support of the IPA. Mitch Fifield told the council that privatisation was not government policy. Then-treasurer Scott Morrison added, to much appreciative chortling in the ranks, that some Australians 'may think the Labor Party already owns it'.

Privatisation may be off the agenda. But there are other ways to skin a cat.

Early in 2018, partly as a result of a deal done to get One Nation's support for legislation that loosened the rules surrounding media ownership, Fifield announced a 'competitive neutrality review' to ask whether the ABC and SBS were exploiting their government funding to compete unfairly in the online space with other news providers. Aunty's commercial rivals took full advantage of the opportunity. Fairfax Media's submission, for example, suggested that the ABC should be restricted to supplying online only those services that are not commercially viable—regional and rural news and views, specialist science, arts and religious affairs.[7]

The reviewing panel, headed by economist Robert Kerr, rejected those arguments. Its report, tabled last December, made clear that the ABC's and SBS's online activities were covered by their charters, and found that 'the National Broadcasters are not causing significant competitive distortions beyond the public interest'.[8]

Round one to the ABC and SBS. But the Turnbull government went further in its efforts to cosy up to One Nation. It introduced several bills to amend the ABC Act: among them, the ABC Amendment (Fair and Balanced) Bill 2017. The ABC Act already requires the board to ensure that the Corporation's news and information is 'accurate and impartial'. The new bill would change those words to 'fair, balanced, accurate and impartial'.[9]

That might sound reasonable. It is not. It is fashioning a stick with which every harebrained fanatic can beat the ABC. One of One Nation's then senators—since booted out by the High Court because he had not renounced his British citizenship before being nominated as a parliamentary candidate—was Malcolm Roberts, who fervently believes that climate change is more than a hoax: it is a plot to yield world government to the United Nations. Roberts will be nominated again as a One Nation candidate for the Senate in the 2019 general election.

If the new bill ever became law, you can be sure that Roberts and his ilk would be demanding that every discussion of climate change should be 'balanced' between the scientific consensus and conspiratorial garbage. The anti-vaxxers would insist that any advocacy for immunisation—arguably the single most effective public health measure since the Victorians installed underground sewers—should be 'balanced' with warnings about alleged risks of autism that have no scientific validity whatsoever.

Fortunately, the cross-bench senators have refused to pass the bill. But it is still sitting there, waiting its moment.

Then, like the Howard and Abbott governments, the Turnbull government pulled out the fiscal razor. The 2018 budget contained a provision that the ABC's funding would no longer be indexed, as promised, against inflation. That amounts to an $84 million cut over the next three years, on top of the $240 million cut imposed in 2014. The new cut came, as acting managing director David Anderson put it in a recent speech, with the 'customary side order of an efficiency review'—yes, another one, this time headed up by Peter Tonagh, fresh from a long career at News Corp.

Jim Middleton, the ABC's political editor for twenty years and now a senior aide to independent Senator Tim Storer, told me that nothing in his long experience compares with the assault since 2014 on the ABC's funding. He described it as 'persistent financial intimidation—a genuine attempt to chop the arms and legs off the ability of the ABC to live up to its charter responsibilities'.

Meanwhile, Fifield and Turnbull have revived another device pioneered by John Howard's minister for communications, Richard Alston: the formal complaint.

In May 2003, Alston made 68 formal complaints about alleged anti-coalition bias in the coverage of the invasion of Iraq by one ABC radio program, *AM*. Over the succeeding two years those complaints wound their way through the many layers of the ABC's complaints handling process: its internal

Complaints Review Executive; its external Independent Complaints Review Panel (ICRP) (ironically, set up in response to the Hawke government's complaints after the first Gulf War); and finally, the Australian Broadcasting Authority (from July 2005 rebadged as the Australian Communications and Media Authority). At each stage, more of Alston's complaints were found to be valid: he ended up winning more than a third of them. *AM*'s primary sin, according to the ICRP and ACMA: it was too openly sceptical of the trustworthiness of the US military's media briefings.[10]

Seriously?

As usual, the public had much more faith in the national broadcaster than did the politicians. A News Limited Newspoll found that

90 per cent of respondents thought the ABC's news and current affairs was 'balanced and even-handed'. Of 44 000 complaints that the ABC received in 2003, only 291 concerned its coverage of the war. They were split almost exactly fifty-fifty between those who thought the ABC displayed a bias in favour of the US-led coalition, and those with the opposite complaint.[11]

Late in 2017, Turnbull and Fifield began using the Alston ploy with unprecedented frequency. Triple j's decision not to run its Hottest 100 on Australia Day triggered a formal complaint from Fifield. The board stuck by triple j. *Tonightly*'s Tom Ballard also copped a complaint from Fifield, for calling a politician a cunt. Even the ACMA rejected that one—considering the audience it was aimed at, found ACMA, the c-word didn't breach the ABC's editorial policies.

Fifield wasn't impressed; and nor was ABC chair, Justin Milne, who on both these issues took the side of the government, quite openly.

In her submission to the Senate inquiry, Michelle Guthrie accused Milne of telling triple j staff, in a meeting held without her knowledge, that 'Malcolm will go ballistic' if they moved the Hottest 100 from Australia Day.[12]

This turns out not to be true. In fact, in mid-October 2017, Milne held a meeting in his own office on the fourteenth floor of the ABC's Ultimo HQ. Present were Michael Mason, then director of radio; Chris Scaddan, the ABC's head of music; Ollie

Wards, content director of triple j; and Michelle Guthrie herself.

The meeting was dominated by Justin Milne, who told the radio executives that the date change—which Wards and Scaddan had been working on, with the full knowledge and apparent endorsement of Guthrie, for a year—was not to go ahead. It was not the ABC's job, Milne told them, to put itself at the forefront of social change. He told them he had been reading about Galileo, who rightly insisted that the earth went around the sun, but was burnt at the stake for his pains. 'You don't want to be burnt at the stake for this,' he told them. (Milne needs to work on his accuracy: the Inquisition forced Galileo to recant his 'heresy', and put him under house arrest until he died a natural death a decade later.)

Besides, Milne told them, in what was to become a familiar refrain, he and Guthrie had to look at the big picture. The decision would antagonise a government that he was trying to persuade to put up hundreds of millions of dollars for new digital infrastructure. Wards doesn't remember a reference to 'Malcolm' going 'ballistic'. According to him, Milne said: 'Malcolm will call me and tell me I'm crazy.'

To the surprise of the radio managers, Michelle Guthrie said hardly a word throughout the meeting. In fact, months later, Michael Mason appears to have forgotten that she was even there. When he described Milne's intervention to Guthrie in August 2018, he implied that she wasn't present. Guthrie (who now says she remembers the October meeting quite well) assumed that Mason was talking about some other occasion when the chair had gone behind her back.

Guthrie didn't mention the October meeting to the Senate inquiry—though Justin Milne certainly did. His evidence was that he and Guthrie had met with triple j staff to talk about the Hottest 100 issue; but he had no recollection of talking to them in her absence. That's not surprising, because according to Ollie Wards (who should know) he never did.

In the end, after some energetic lobbying, the board overruled Milne by a single vote. In defiance of the government's complaint, the date change went ahead.

But Fifield and Turnbull were only getting started—and the chair of the ABC would be with them all the way.

'Get rid of her'

Emma Alberici is an experienced television and radio journalist. She'd been one of the ABC's Europe correspondents, based in London, then had been a presenter for *Lateline* for five years. When *Lateline* was closed down in 2017, she was offered, and accepted, the job of 'chief economics correspondent', nominally under the supervision of business editor Ian Verrender.

Her two articles on the government's corporate tax cuts policy—one news story, the other labelled 'analysis'—hit the ABC website in the early hours of 14 February 2018. Before 8 a.m., ABC director of news Gaven Morris was asking his deputy if they had been fact-checked. Justin Milne was wondering (in an email to Morris) whether the analysis piece was 'balanced'. Within hours, the ABC received written complaints from the prime minister's office, backed by the minister for communications, and Treasury. In due course, Qantas and the Business Council of Australia joined the queue of complainants.

The news story did contain errors—nine of them in all, though most were minor. The biggest problems were with the headline and 'teasers', none written by Alberici, which gave the impression that some of Australia's biggest companies were involved in illegal tax evasion. Those errors were rapidly corrected. Importantly, the ABC's Audience and Consumer Affairs department rejected a claim that was repeatedly made in the media: that Alberici had made the elementary error of confusing revenue with profit. In fact, it rejected most of the complaints it received about the news story.

The analysis piece, however, was taken down completely. It took the ABC more than a week to re-post a substantially rewritten piece.

The timing didn't help. Corporate tax cuts constituted the Turnbull government's most significant economic policy measure. At that moment, it was trying desperately to persuade cross-bench senators to pass them into law. Links to Alberici's 'analysis' were being triumphantly tweeted by the opposition front bench. No wonder the government went feral.

Yet Alberici had submitted the piece to both the business and the analysis editors, and both had approved it. So Justin Milne and the board were completely justified in asking how either piece had got through the system. News management was asking the same question.

The fact is that the ABC's editorial processes were honed in the pre-digital era, when what it produced was television and radio reports. Generally, these consist of interview grabs linked by a sentence or two of the reporter's narration. Now ABC reporters—especially its specialist correspondents—are expected to produce online 'analysis' that can often extend to thousands of words.

Rigorous fact-checking by several pairs of eyes is routine on programs like *Four Corners* and *Media Watch*. There simply isn't the manpower to do the same for every online story. And the facts aren't the only problem.

In commercial news media, analysis by their own reporters is often fiercely opinionated. On the ABC, it can't be. ABC reporters are required to produce 'analysis', not 'opinion'. The ABC's editorial gurus have produced pages of Guidance notes about how reporters and editors can distinguish between the two.[13] But in the end, it's a matter of judgement.

The ABC admitted that in its original form, Alberici's 'analysis' wasn't an impartial appraisal of the merits of corporate tax cuts. It was a fiercely argued piece rubbishing the government's claim that they would lead to increased wages. There was no shortage of expert commentary elsewhere that agreed with that argument. But, pronounced Audience and Consumer Affairs, what she had written was opinion, not analysis.

Since then, every substantial or potentially controversial online analysis piece produced by the News Division has had to be OK'd by its second-most senior executive, deputy director Craig McMurtrie. It is far from an ideal solution. It has caused logjams to build up. But it's one of the prices to be paid for the ABC's venture into the world of text-based journalism.

Michelle Guthrie was in theory the Corporation's editor-in-chief. In one sense, the title is simply an acknowledgement of the reality that the buck for everything the ABC publishes stops at the MD's desk. But nothing in Guthrie's professional background—or in that of plenty of other managing directors, including Russell Balding, Jonathan Shier and David Hill—equipped her to second-guess the professional journalists who reported to her. So far as I can judge, she relied, as she was bound to, on the judgement of her news director, Gaven Morris, and editorial director, Alan Sunderland—whose brief is to ensure that the ABC's entire output accords with its editorial policies.

They would have known—and so did Guthrie—that though the ABC's reputation for accuracy and impartiality is precious, it's not secured by sacking journalists who make mistakes. And indeed, the Fair Work Commission would probably have ruled that dismissal in such a case would have been (in a legal sense) unfair.

But in Justin Milne's view, apparently, those minor errors, and Alberici's crossing of the always-vague line between opinion and analysis, rendered her all but unemployable. For him, the Corporation's entire survival was in play. He believed that its future depended on the massive digital infrastructure upgrade he had dubbed 'Project Jetstream'. He reckoned it would cost half a billion dollars—money he was trying to persuade the government to spend upfront, in exchange for savings many years down the track.

Milne is a businessman, and in business you keep your investors happy. Alberici's articles—to which *The Australian* and the *Australian Financial Review* were devoting a marathon of outraged column inches—were making the ABC's sole potential investor very unhappy. 'Our chances of getting extra money,' he emailed to the board on

20 February, 'or perhaps even maintaining our current funding, may have been significantly diminished by this issue.'[14]

A conduit, not a wall.

Three months later, just two days before the budget, Alberici filed a television story for *7.30* on Australia's poor record as an innovative economy. The next day, for the fifth time in as many months, Mitch Fifield weighed in with a hefty government complaint.

When Michelle Guthrie forwarded its substance to Justin Milne on 8 May, budget day, she tried to indicate that in her view, Fifield was using any stick he could find with which to beat the ABC, 'partic Emma'.

But that evening, as reporters streamed out of the budget lock-up, Justin Milne felt that his dire predictions of the previous February had come to pass: no extra money for ABC digital infrastructure, and an unheralded three-year indexation freeze—an effective $84 million cut.

And to make matters worse, thought Milne, Alberici was hoeing into the government again. That evening (after 'a few glasses of red', he admitted) he sent the now-notorious email to Guthrie: 'They fricken hate her … She keeps sticking it to them with a clear bias against them. We clear her as OK. We r tarred with her brush. I just think it's simple. Get rid of her. My view is we need to save the corporation, not Emma.'

In fact, Alberici's innovation analysis was a perfectly respectable and relevant piece. Two weeks later, the ABC's Audience and

Consumer Affairs department rejected all the government's complaints, except one—an academic Alberici had described as a government consultant was actually working for a bipartisan Senate committee. Of course Alberici's piece criticised some aspects of government policy. But that's what journalists do. To regard it as work deserving of dismissal was bizarre.

But it wasn't he who first contemplated 'getting rid' of Alberici, Milne told the Senate inquiry.[15] His notorious email—which he admitted was 'intemperate'—should be read, he testified, in the context of negotiations between Alberici and senior management that had been going on for months. He understood that Guthrie and news director Gaven Morris were trying to persuade Alberici to move to a different job—or even to leave the ABC altogether. The 'external development opportunity', Milne called it—a euphemism, he told *Four Corners*, for the sack.[16]

Guthrie and Morris maintain that's not what it meant. They were discussing Alberici's career options, that's all.[17] Well, whatever, the government's renewed attack made it politically impossible for Alberici to be moved: as Guthrie and Morris saw clearly, if Milne did not, it would have looked as if the ABC was buckling to government pressure.

Alberici is still chief economics correspondent. Justin Milne is no longer chair. We may never know if Malcolm Turnbull and Mitch Fifield 'fricken hated' Alberici enough to urge Milne to 'get rid of her'. I'm inclined to believe not, at least directly. But certainly

Turnbull has demonstrated while in office, and since he left, that he has as fragile a glass jaw as any of his predecessors. The scale of the government's attack on Alberici, multiplied many times over by its gleeful accessories at *The Australian* and the *Australian Financial Review*, was out of all proportion to her journalistic sins.

But the sheer petulance of the government's attacks on the ABC's journalism didn't reach its zenith with Alberici. For that we have to look at its assault on political editor Andrew Probyn.

'You have to shoot him'

He's universally known around Parliament House as 'Probes'.

The press gallery offices are on the second floor of the Senate wing of new Parliament House. It's a building where the corridors of power are wide and spacious, the doors high and elegant, the parquet floors polished and gleaming. But nowhere else in Australia are reporters so routinely castigated in such inelegant terms.

The hundreds of journalists in the gallery are usually chasing the same few stories each day. The place thrives on leaks, drops, rumours, steers, tips, backgrounders, hints and denials. 'Off the record', 'background' or 'deep background' is how this dubious information is traded—by frontbenchers and backbenchers, aides and advisors, and even the odd public servant. On the record statements are much less common, though just as likely to be half-true or even false.

The habitués of this disconcerting milieu have their bosses, too—editors who know the sort of stories their readers want, or their proprietors want, or both. That knowledge, too, is weighed in the balance, consciously or not, as gallery reporters decide what to post or what to air.

It's without doubt the most testing and competitive journalistic environment in the country. You need experience, judgement and an excellent nose for bullshit to come up with a story that's more true than not—and a very thick hide. Language that's routine here would barely be tolerated in any other workplace. 'They'll get on the phone and scream at you: "Fuck you, you pathetic wanker, who do you think you are? We'll fucking get you for this!"—that's the way politics is played here. It's the way they treat each other. It's routine. You shrug it off. They'll be briefing you again next day,' another old hand told me.

The ABC has always copped it from the politicians: a lot of them reckon they own it; and all of them know it won't bite back the way some of the private empires do. But according to five separate sources, 2018 was one of the toughest years in recent memory—and at the heart of it was Probes.

Andrew Probyn is an experienced gallery reporter who worked for a decade for Kerry Stokes's *The West Australian*. During the 2016 election campaign he broke a story for *The West* about how the Liberals were planning to privatise the payment system for Medicare. That was true, at the time, though the plan was abandoned in the face of the unrelenting scare campaign that almost won Labor the election: Bill Shorten claimed that Turnbull was planning to privatise Medicare itself.

That wasn't true, and it wasn't what Probyn's story had said. But in the view of many in the gallery, the Medicare payments story earned him the undying hatred of Turnbull's office, and especially of his chief of staff, Sally Cray. 'She said it showed he was working for Labor,' one gallery veteran said—a ludicrous idea to those who know Probyn. 'You could not get anyone more centrist and non-political,' a close colleague of Probyn's told me. 'There are some very political people around here and Probes is not one of them.'

Ludicrous it might be, unusual it's not. Between the political and the journalistic world view there's an all-but-unbridgeable chasm. What is important to journalists, whoever they work for and whatever medium they work in, is the 'story'. It's a word so commonly used in the trade that reporters don't need to define it; and indeed, it's used to describe everything from a single article on page five of the local paper, to an event that the world's press is pursuing. A 'good' story is a story that people will want to read, that makes an impact, that hasn't been told before: it's the grail that every journo pursues.

The mind of the mainstream politician, especially if he or she is a member of one of the two major parties, is different. It's a Manicheistic world, of our side (good), and their side (bad): those who are not for us are against us—and that means they are working for the other lot. Two-party politics is a tennis match, played with ruthless concentration. Journalists—especially if they're from the ABC, with its duty of 'impartiality'—are thought of as commentators. If they stop merely calling the match, and start giving their listeners behind-the-scenes details that favour one side more than the other, by definition, regardless of whether the story is true or not, they are biased.

In early 2017, Andrew Probyn, already marked by Turnbull's office as 'biased' to Labor, accepted an offer to become the chief political correspondent for the ABC's *7.30*.

It's just a short walk down the corridor from *The West*'s cramped office in Parliament House to the 35-strong ABC bureau. But as Probyn would find, there's a dramatic difference between writing for a newspaper whose readership is mainly confined to a single state, and appearing nightly on a television channel that is beamed into every home in the land. There is an even bigger difference between working for a commercial media company, and for a public broadcaster with statutory obligations to accuracy and impartiality.

The politicians allow some liberties to be taken by *7.30*'s chief political correspondent—as do the regulators, internal and external. Not nearly as many, mind you, as Richard Carleton took every evening on the ABC's *Nationwide* in the early 1980s. Newly arrived from the UK, I remember being gobsmacked by the ferocity of Carleton's commentary on politics, and politicians. No one at the BBC was allowed such latitude—and nobody at the ABC is allowed it today.

Still, Probyn's editors in Sydney would have been encouraging him to push the boundaries. *7.30*'s political correspondent often has to comment on the same events that *ABC News* has reported half an hour earlier. *7.30* looks for more caustic, or wittier, or more insightful analysis than the news is permitted to offer. But no sooner had Probyn begun to find his feet at *7.30*, than he was switched to the big job, political editor of ABC News.

He discovered quite quickly how much less leeway is granted there. Michelle Guthrie told the Senate committee that as early as AFL Grand Final Day, 30 September 2017, the prime minister approached her at the pre-match lunch at the MCG and dropped into the conversation his dissatisfaction with Andrew Probyn's reporting. What Malcolm Turnbull's specific grouses were, Guthrie didn't say, and perhaps Turnbull didn't tell her. But already, the pressure was on.[18]

Then, on 10 October, Probyn reported on a speech that Tony Abbott had just made to a gathering of climate sceptics in London. In a piece to camera on *ABC News* at 7 p.m.

Probyn commented: 'Tony Abbott, already the most destructive politician of his generation, now intends waging war on what he calls "environmental theology". If this tells us anything, it's that Malcolm Turnbull can't do anything to appease Tony Abbott on climate action.'

An anonymous viewer complained to the ABC that this was opinion, not news. The ABC knocked back the complaint: it was analysis, it found. The complainant wasn't satisfied, and went to the ACMA. Seven months after the story went to air, the regulator delivered its finding. To describe Abbott as 'already the most destructive politician of his generation' was, it found, 'a declarative statement which was incongruent with the substance and scope of the factual matters presented earlier in the report ... It was not in keeping with the ABC's requirement to present the news with due impartiality'.[19]

For what it's worth, *Media Watch*'s Paul Barry agreed with the ACMA. Probyn had taken 'a step too far'.[20]

It would have been easy to avoid getting pinged. Just a couple of words would have done the trick. 'Tony Abbott, already regarded even by many in his own party as a destructive force' would have been fine, because it's undeniably true—reportage rather than analysis. Not quite as forceful, perhaps, but much safer.

It's the sort of phrasing that experienced ABC reporters would adopt almost without thinking. Probyn was learning the hard way. For the next few months, according to his colleagues inside and outside the ABC bureau, the pressure on Probyn, mainly from the prime minister's office, was 'sustained, and personal, and all-consuming'. One of the few prepared to go on the record is Probyn's predecessor in the ABC job, Chris Uhlmann, now political editor at the Nine Network. 'Sally Cray, Malcolm's spear carrier, launched a barrage of complaints about him, to his bureau chief and to [ABC news director] Gaven Morris. There were streams of messages to the bureau from others in the PM's office; a What'sApp barrage that was constantly picking holes.'

Then, on 25 May, in the middle of a routine story on the *ABC News*, filling a hole in the 7 p.m. bulletin on a Friday night, Probyn indulged in what he now calls a bit of 'journalese'. Labor was 'squeezed', he said in a piece to camera, by 'the prime minister's decision to time [the] Super Saturday [by-elections] with a long-scheduled Labor national conference'.

Mitch Fifield's complaint—the sixth in five months—dropped on the ABC a few days later; and it didn't stop with Andrew Probyn. It named four more of the press gallery's most senior reporters and commentators: Laura Tingle of the ABC's *7.30*; Barrie Cassidy of *Insiders*; Phil Coorey of the *Australian Financial Review*; and Mark Kenny of Fairfax Media. All had had the temerity to state on the ABC that the prime minister, or the government, had decided the date of the by-elections. This, claimed Fifield, is 'a Labor lie'. Probyn and Tingle should not have repeated it, and Barrie Cassidy should have challenged Kenny and Coorey when they made the same claim on *Insiders*.

The ABC conceded, rightly, that Probyn should not have ascribed the decision to the prime minister in a television news bulletin—or at least should have included his denial. It rejected the other complaints.

Fifield had overreached. All these veteran correspondents knew perfectly well that the speaker does not make these decisions without consulting the government. Coorey, Kenny, Cassidy and Tingle, as well as Probyn, all had contacts in the coalition who assured them that the disruption to Labor's national conference, though it may not have been the main reason for the choice of date, was regarded as a bonus by the government. As

Laura Tingle wrote on 9 June: 'On the day the date of the by-elections was announced by House Speaker Tony Smith, senior cabinet ministers were joking with journalists about the fact the date would play havoc with Labor's planned national conference.' As for Fifield's complaints, Tingle reported, 'people inside the coalition' had explained to her that 'you've got to play to the base'.[21]

Both Tingle and Probyn are seasoned gallery correspondents who only recently arrived at the ABC from commercial media. Both were struck by the partisan use to which the ABC's elaborate complaints procedures were put by the Turnbull government. Andrew Probyn told me: 'The ABC is like that puny kid in the playground, easy to bash up because it's largely defenceless, because of all these ways in which we open ourselves up for scrutiny. That has got great benefits for ordinary consumers—readers, listeners, viewers—[who want] to question our journalism or facts or a slant that they don't like; but the same mechanisms can be used by government, and that's what they've been doing.'

Laura Tingle criticised what she called 'the culture of the coalition' on *Insiders* on the weekend after Milne's resignation: 'OK we're a taxpayer-funded body and we have a higher level of accountability for what we do, completely understood—but the extent to which people in the coalition felt that they could bully, harangue and harass journalists, and the management of the ABC, about issues on a day-to-day basis has been quite shocking to see for somebody who has worked in all the media organisations: I worked at News, I worked at Fairfax, and it is a completely different cultural relationship.'[22]

Probyn's 'journalese' on 25 May was sloppy. But most prime ministers wouldn't have thought it worth more than a furious phone call. When Justin Milne came to Parliament House on 15 June to talk to Turnbull and Fifield about Jetstream, he was advised by the ABC bureau not to worry about the Probyn complaint: a storm in a teacup. But the politicians, it seems, were still steaming. At any rate, that same day, Milne rang Guthrie and, as she insisted to the Senate inquiry, yelled at her about Probyn.

Once again, we'll probably never know what passed between Turnbull, Fifield and Milne. Did the politicians make it clear that if

Milne was to have any hope of getting his half billion dollars for Jetstream, he would have to make sure that the ABC cleaned up its act—starting with Andrew Probyn? Possibly: such things can be conveyed without being stated in so many words. If Probyn's name came up at all, in a conversation that was ostensibly about funding digital infrastructure, it would surely have been hint enough.

Milne says that nobody in government ever asked him to get rid of individual journalists; that he never mentioned Andrew Probyn to Guthrie when he called that afternoon; that Guthrie has invented the conversation she describes. Guthrie is adamant that Milne told her to 'shoot' Probyn, that he yelled at her, that she was left shaken and close to tears.

I report, you decide, as Fox News would put it. But if Guthrie's version is true, it's hard to believe that Milne conjured Probyn's name out of the blue. Like a reliable conduit, he was passing on—and doubtless, in Guthrie's word, 'amplifying'—a message received.

Bias, balance and the base

Whatever Sally Cray might have said about Andrew Probyn, Malcolm Turnbull insists that he never complained about political bias. 'A lot of politicians do,' he told *Q&A*'s audience in November 2018, months after his resignation. 'I'd given up on that years ago. You've got to be realistic. But I do think that now, more than ever, the ABC needs to adhere to its charter and its statutory obligation in its own Act of delivering news and current affairs which is accurate and objective, consistent with the standards of objective journalism.'

Turnbull nearly got it right. According to the ABC Act, the board has a duty 'to ensure that the gathering and presentation by the Corporation of news and information is accurate and impartial according to the recognized standards of objective journalism'.

There were inaccuracies in Emma Alberici's reports. There shouldn't have been. Probyn shouldn't have made the bald statement in a news report that the prime minister chose the date of by-elections. But to blow up these comparatively minor errors and misjudgements to the extent that the government did is doing just what Laura Tingle was told it is: 'playing to the base'.

Ah, the Liberal party base. The supposed wishes and grumbles, prejudices and foibles of this extraordinarily powerful group of voters have dominated Australia's politics for almost a decade. Because of the base,

Australia has no climate change policy—though the broader public wants one. If the base had had its way, we would have no same-sex marriage: we had to go through a painful and unnecessary plebiscite to get around the base's blockade. The base loathed Malcolm Turnbull, so he had to go—to the fury of the Liberal voters of Wentworth, and perhaps (we shall see) of Australia. And if it were up to the base, the ABC would go too.

The Liberal party base represents, at most, 25 per cent of the population—probably less. But to the base, the ABC is irretrievably, hopelessly, shamefully biased.

The Australian, for commercial as well as ideological reasons, has been the ABC's most vocal media critic for at least thirty years; recently, it has become more strident than ever. In the week that Guthrie was ousted and Milne resigned, its editor-at-large, Paul Kelly, posed a series of questions to those who claim the ABC is impartial:

> Didn't the ABC display a strong preference for same-sex marriage? Wasn't it critical of border protection measures to stop asylum-seeker boats? Doesn't it favour strong action on climate change and criticise governments for not being sufficiently ambitious? Doesn't it project support for renewables and faster efforts to phase out fossil fuels? Wasn't the ABC distinctly unsympathetic to the policy of corporate tax cuts? Wasn't it hostile towards reform of section 18C of the Racial Discrimination Act and unsympathetic to free speech arguments? Doesn't it push for a referendum on an indigenous voice to

parliament and criticise government over this? Isn't it uncritical of social spending programs and critical of cuts to such programs in the cause of fiscal discipline? Isn't it more focused on inequality than economic growth and more supportive of government intervention over market forces?[23]

To which the standard ABC response is 'no, no and no—the ABC has no editorial position'. But anyone who works there knows this is disingenuous. Line up any hundred ABC staffers and ask them those questions, substituting 'you' for 'it'. 'Don't you have a strong preference for same-sex marriage? Aren't you critical of border protection measures?'—and so on down the list. If they're honest, at least eighty will answer 'yes, yes, yes and yes'.

It's a problem more easily identified than solved. The fact is that the sort of bright young people who want to work at the ABC are going to incline to the left, just as those who line up to be investment bankers or market traders are more likely to incline to the right.

ABC staffers have also, until very recently, been overwhelmingly white and middle class. The whiteness can legitimately be addressed by conscious policies to recruit for ethnic diversity—one of Michelle Guthrie's priorities. But surely the ABC can't make political inclination a selection criterion for recruitment? That's to embark on a perilous path.

Of course, none of this would be a problem, if the ABC were a commercial media organisation. As Paul Kelly pointed out:

These days every media organisation has an editorial culture—just think of CNN, *The Wall Street Journal*, *The New York Times*, Fox News, *The Daily Telegraph*, *The Guardian*, the Macquarie radio network, *Breitbart*, *The Australian* and Sky News, to list names at random. Which one is politically impartial? None. This leads to the obvious question: in a time when politics defines the market position of a media organisation, how can the ABC be impartial, and how long can it continue the pretence that it is?

This is the real dilemma of the public broadcaster under a legislated charter purporting to be free of bias. You cannot square the circle. It doesn't fit any more. The hoax becomes more and more absurd. Knowing your audience means knowing their demographics and their politics. It's about being professional.[24]

What Kelly is saying (I think) is that in the partisan world of modern media, and modern politics, there is simply no space for the ideal of impartiality 'according to the recognized standards of objective journalism'—and therefore no place for a public broadcaster.

And certainly, in the United States, where the concept was born a century ago, the very notion of 'objective journalism' is being challenged from both sides of the bitter partisan divide.

PBS, the Public Broadcasting System, still clings to the ideal of objectivity—but compared to the ABC in Australia or the BBC in Britain, PBS is a marginal player. CNN, the

New York Times, indeed most of the mainstream media still profess to be 'objective'. But American conservatives, led by Donald Trump, deride the notion that they are. They are 'enemies of the people', 'the liberal media', purveyors of 'fake news'.

The criticism of 'objectivity' comes from the left too. Professor Jay Rosen of New York University, one of the left's favourite media pundits, argues that the pursuit of 'impartiality' and 'balance' has led to what he calls 'the view from nowhere', in which journalists have convinced themselves that it isn't their job, when reporting on a matter of dispute, to research and report on who's right, and who's wrong: if they report on what he said, and what she said, fairly and objectively, they reckon they have done their job.[25]

In a celebrated exchange a few years back, Bill Keller, a former editor-in-chief of *The New York Times*, discussed the ideal of objectivity with Glenn Greenwald, the fiery lawyer-turned-blogger-turned-reporter who first published Edward Snowden's revelations about the surveillance state. Since then, Greenwald has left *The Guardian*, and the United States. He now writes from his base in Brazil for a crusading website, *The Intercept*, financed by eBay billionaire Pierre Omidyar.

Greenwald has never had any time for the ideals of objectivity and balance. 'This suffocating constraint', he wrote to Keller, 'produces a self-neutering form of journalism that becomes as ineffectual as it is boring … Lazily equating a demonstrably true assertion with a demonstrably false one drains journalism of its passion, vibrancy, vitality and soul.' Besides, he argues, no one is truly objective. We all have subjective opinions. 'The relevant distinction is between journalists who honestly disclose their subjective assumptions and political values and those who dishonestly pretend they have none or conceal them from their readers.'

To which Bill Keller responded: 'I don't think of it as reporters pretending they have no opinions. I think of it as reporters, as an occupational discipline, suspending their opinions and letting the evidence speak for itself. And it matters that this is not just an individual exercise, but an institutional discipline, with editors who are tasked to challenge writers if they have given short shrift to contrary facts or arguments readers might want to know.'[26]

That's a pretty good description of 'the recognized standards of objective journalism', and if you work for the ABC, you don't have a choice. That's the model you must follow. You are required to sublimate your own opinions—or at least, to do your best to do so. You can certainly provide analysis, based on demonstrable evidence, using unemotional language. But you cannot be an advocate.

And I would argue (though no doubt the ABC's critics would disagree) that in its news bulletins, and to a great extent in its current affairs programs, on television, radio and online text, the ABC manages that pretty well. The Alberici piece on corporate tax cuts was the exception, not the rule.

But the ABC broadcasts and publishes far more than news and current affairs. In her recent book in this series, *On Disruption*, the political editor of *Guardian Australia*, Katharine Murphy, argues that survival, in the digital world, depends on publications like hers creating a community of readers. She quotes Steve Coll, writing in *The New Yorker* in 2017: 'Amid the cacophony of the digital era, publishers and advertisers prize readers who are deeply engaged, not just clicking around sites. News organizations as distinct as *The [New York] Times* and *Breitbart* now think of their audiences as communities in formation, bound by common values.'[27]

To radio people, that's old news. Radio, the most intimate of media, has always known that the secret to success is building a community of like-minded listeners. People who like the same music, be it Mozart and

Beethoven, or old-time swing or free-form jazz or Australian punk. People who share similar political views: the Alan Joneses and Ray Hadleys don't expect to be listened to by those who disagree with them.

But the very fact that so many commercial radio talkback hosts, especially in cities other than Melbourne, have sought to form communities of disgruntled, right-leaning listeners has meant almost inevitably that more progressive talk-radio listeners gravitate towards ABC metropolitan radio. ABC radio presenters know it, and respond to that audience. It's a mutually reinforcing paradigm.

Given the competition on metro talk radio, it is understandable that ABC management hasn't tried to counter this mild leftward tilt. But Radio National, whose ambition is, or should be, to cater for those of all political persuasions who want high-quality information and discussion, has much less excuse for giving Phillip Adams his unique platform.

No doubt the Liberal 'base' (let alone adherents of parties further to the right) think that the likes of Fran Kelly and Patricia Karvelas are 'lefties'. But they try hard to appeal across the party divide. Adams doesn't. Never has. For over twenty years the host of *Late Night Live* has been openly, unapologetically and at times scornfully a man of the left. His 'Gladdies' and 'Poddies' love him for it. He's created his radio community, and holds up two fingers to the very notion of 'impartiality'.

Adams is a consummate broadcaster, supported by a fine team of producers. He's getting long in the tooth for sure, but his guests are still interesting, his interviews stimulating—if you are sympathetic to his values. If you're not, he must be infuriating.

I am not suggesting that Adams should be taken off the air. But surely some manager of Radio National, decades ago, should have said to themselves: 'Just as Phillip has been able to form a community of like-minded progressive listeners, there must be someone in Australia who can form a similar community of like-minded conservatives who don't want to be hectored by the likes of Hadley and Jones.' After all, half the population votes conservative at every election.

But instead, the complaints about Adams have become, for ABC insiders, a joke to be sniggered at. Ken Inglis records in *Whose ABC?* that in 2005, a cartoon on the wall of the director of radio's office showed an empty cage, with the caption: 'Oh Lord! The right-wing Phillip Adams has escaped!'

Admittedly, ABC radio has made attempts to recapture the elusive beast; but not with much enthusiasm or commitment. In the Howard era, Radio National launched *Counterpoint*, hosted these days by former Howard minister Amanda Vanstone—for one hour a week on a Monday afternoon. And Tom Switzer, like Vanstone a liberal Liberal, hosts *Between the Lines* for half an hour a week. Of course, these days Vanstone and Switzer fans can download their podcasts and listen any time. Still, it's a derisory effort.

I talked to a prominent conservative commentator who told me: 'People on the right are just so pissed off. They are angrier than they have ever been, because they don't feel there is anything on the ABC that resonates with them or people like them. They just don't see why they should go on paying for it.'

In response to which the ABC trots out its qualitative surveys—and they are impressive. Poll after poll, by Essential, and Newspoll, and Saulwick, as well as the ABC's own surveys, shows that support for the ABC remains at between 70 and 80 per cent of the population, and that it's the most trusted news source in Australia, by a distance. But the ABC's own surveys also show that the number of those who think that Aunty is doing a poor or very poor job has almost doubled in recent years—from 5 to 10 per cent.

Unfashionable though it may be, the ABC must stick to the ideal of objectivity.

For a public broadcaster, there is no other legal or ethical choice. As for Paul Kelly's assertion that the ABC's pretence to impartiality is a 'hoax [that] becomes more and more absurd', it's clear that only a minority of Australians agree with him. The minority is vocal, passionate and probably beyond appeasing.

Yet it shouldn't be shrugged off, as too many inside the ABC do. It's the same minority, in essence, as that Liberal or conservative 'base' that wields so much influence in the modern coalition. It is crucial that the ABC makes those people, too, feel that somewhere in its output, online or on air, there are places where its views and concerns are heard, and reflected, and, to the extent that the verifiable facts allow, given validity.

Disruptive transformation

This is a short essay, and I have devoted more than half of it to the trials and tribulations of the ABC's political reporting. And yet there is so much more to the ABC—vastly more than there was when I joined it in the early 1980s: kids' programs and drama and documentary and comedy and local radio and Radio National and triple j and double j and Classic FM and Grandstand, let alone the proliferation of online and digital offerings that aren't broadcast at all.

But most politicians don't watch or listen to much of that. They are busy people, and overwhelmingly they are interested in politics.

If they represent rural electorates, they know that the commercial media are struggling, that ABC radio and ABC websites are more crucial than ever as a means of reaching out to their constituents. That's why the National Party remains the best friend the ABC has in the coalition. If they're from city electorates, they know that the ABC is the most trusted news source among the many their constituents consume—so they are hypersensitive to any coverage they perceive as hostile.

This is certainly as true of Labor as of coalition governments. For much of the 1990s, the redoubtable Quentin Dempster was the staff-elected director on the ABC board. In his account of the ABC in that decade, rather melodramatically entitled *Death Struggle*, Dempster describes how the board took stock after the unexpected victory of Paul Keating over John Hewson in March 1993: 'Friends in that particular cabinet were few and far between. It was often reported to the board that when ABC matters were raised in Cabinet, ministers would launch into a barrage of anti-ABC criticism over some heinous piece of misreporting of their individual pronouncements or activities. Substantive issues of vital concern to the ABC and its role in Australian culture and public affairs would be swamped in superficial bile and vituperation.'[28]

A quarter of a century on, nothing has changed. It was to allay that bile and vituperation that Justin Milne suggested to his managing director that Emma Alberici had to go, and (allegedly) that Andrew Probyn be hauled before a firing squad. And, horribly misjudged as his reaction was, there's no reason to doubt that his motive was just as he described it to Leigh Sales on the day of his resignation: 'The role of the chair and the board is to ensure the longevity of the corporation. Now, this organisation, like all other media organisations, is under significant threat, really … from the fact that technology is changing … The ABC has to build digital infrastructure for the future. That's going to cost a lot of money, my estimation about half a billion dollars.'[29]

Milne was obsessed, to requote Quentin Dempster, with a 'substantive issue of vital concern to the ABC and its role in Australian culture and public affairs'—in fact, with its future survival. So was Michelle Guthrie. So is every ABC board member, every senior manager, every program-maker and bean counter and marketer and data analyst in the corporation.

Like every other media organisation worldwide, the ABC is a victim of digital disruption. It is seeing the audience on its traditional platforms—in its case, broadcast radio and television—become smaller, and older, year by year. In earlier eras, Australians under the age of twelve, and their parents, would be avid consumers of the ABC, be it *The Argonauts* or *Play School* or *Mr Squiggle*. The creation of triple j in the 1970s enabled the ABC to hang on to an audience in their teens and twenties that had earlier simply deserted the national broadcaster. But in their thirties and forties—the age at which most Australians in the twentieth century would begin to subscribe to a daily newspaper—they would also return to

ABC news and current affairs, to ABC television and radio in general.

But no one in their teens or twenties, and very few in their thirties and forties, watches live television any more, unless it's to watch sport, from which the ABC has been priced out, or they are enticed there by a second screen. To vote for or against a contestant in a 'reality' contest, or to see your own tweet on *Q&A*, you have to be watching live. For everything else, there's catch-up streaming or YouTube. For music, there's Spotify and its ilk. Even viewers in their seventies and eighties are likely to time-shift their favourite programs—especially on commercial channels, so they can speed through the ads.

And there is so much else available to amuse us. Video games, and binge-watching fabulously expensive drama on Netflix and Stan, and the world's finest news sites and magazines for a few dollars a month, or none at all, not to mention the ever-present lure of social media, which chews up hours of our time, whether we are ten or eighty-five. And instead of broadcast radio, we all carry in our pockets a device that can access at a touch highly produced audio podcasts on every topic under the sun, not to mention almost every music recording ever made. If they are not free—and most of them are—they are as cheap as chips.

None of these people are ever going to come back to watching broadcast television or listening to particular radio programs at an appointed hour. For the free-to-air commercial broadcasters, this is a crisis that is destroying the simple business model that made them, for fifty-odd years, some of the most profitable companies in Australia: make programs that people want to watch, and sell the eyeballs of your captive audience to advertisers.

Like newspapers, it will take a decade or more for commercial broadcast television to become entirely unviable. But it will happen. (Radio, a much cheaper medium, might last longer.) As Australia's advertising spend switches from print and television to online, almost all the growth is going not to companies that produce original news or entertainment, but to the supranational tech behemoths, especially Google and Facebook.

For the ABC, the crisis is not quite so immediate. It still gets a billion dollars of taxpayers' money per year, as the Turnbull and Morrison governments have endlessly reminded us. That figure has been chopped and chipped away at for three decades—in real dollar terms, the ABC's budget is barely half what it was in the 1980s. But compared with the collapse in revenue faced by the likes of Fairfax Media, News Corp or even Seven West, the public broadcasters have it easy.

But they still have to face the fact that the audience for broadcast television, in particular, is plummeting. ABC news director Gaven Morris told me: 'In the past ten years, the 7 o'clock news has lost 40 per cent of its audience and the average age of its viewers has gone up by ten years. If you look at the audience for news and current affairs on the main ABC channel, the average age is seventy.'

When Mark Scott arrived from Fairfax Media in 2006, he was deeply conscious of the need for the ABC to become digitally literate. But it was not yet a matter of survival. Much of his energy, and of the savings that new technology was making possible, were poured into the additional television channels that digital broadcasting made room for in the spectrum—ABC Kids, and ABC 2, and especially ABC News 24 (now ABC News Channel). To some of us it seemed—and still seems—that, after a failed attempt to launch a 24-hour news channel back in the 1990s, the ABC finally arrived at 24-hour news just as it was becoming irrelevant. News 24 launched in 2010. Apple's iPhone had been on the market for three years. Smartphones were becoming universal. If people wanted access to 24-hour news, they didn't want to sit down in front of their television sets to do it. They wanted it right there, in the palms of their hands.

With the launch of iview, Scott was right on the money. The ABC was way in front of the commercial channels with its catch-up service. It could be accessed on tablets and smart phones as well as television sets. It released viewers from the schedule, and from their living room television sets.

All this innovation and expansion costs money. Certainly, modern technology, combined with staff multi-skilling, has made possible some radical downsizing in production departments. The ABC was able to fund much of its digital expansion under Scott—including News 24—by sometimes drastic pruning elsewhere. And the Rudd and Gillard governments found a few tens of millions to fund, for example, an expansion of rural and regional coverage on radio and online. But then came the Abbott-Hockey budget of 2014. Abbott's promise not to cut the ABC's funding was blatantly broken.

The infamous 'hunger games' round of redundancies followed. Programs were dropped—including, in 2016, the last vestige of state-based current affairs, when *7.30*'s Friday edition was abolished. And behind the scenes, the all-important software spend fell behind. ABC iview, once a pioneer, was allowed to become clunky and outdated. Compared with Netflix and Stan, and even Freeview and SBS On Demand, iview was difficult to search. It required no sign-in, so it didn't recognise the user. It couldn't suggest programs you might have liked to watch, or let you pick up viewing a program where you left off.

Most of these problems with iview have now, belatedly, been fixed. The content management system has not. A good CMS is crucial to any media organisation that wants to post content smoothly, efficiently and attractively online. I lost count of the number of program-makers, in the News Division and beyond, who told me that the ABC's CMS is hard to use, and a decade behind its rivals' systems. There is a desperate need for software templates that any journalist can use to post their own stories and pictures online without needing a degree in coding. No one has been tasked with the job, or given the budget to produce them. The hard-pressed online news people in Brisbane, trying to fill their own hungry beast every day, are constantly called on to help program-makers in *Foreign Correspondent* or *Background Briefing* and any number of other programs to produce online stories that can feature on the ABC's main news site—where far more readers would see it than if it were confined to the programs' own sites.

Some ABC people told me that the only real option is to scrap the CMS and start again—as the BBC did not long ago, and Fairfax Media too. Trying to patch up a bad purchase never really works—partly because the more you patch and repair, the harder it is to make smooth transitions to upgrades as they become available. But to start again would cost tens of millions, at the very least.

These were just some of the problems facing Michelle Guthrie when she arrived at the ABC in May 2016.

She was hired as a change-agent, a disruptor. She had managed Star TV in Hong Kong for Rupert Murdoch. She'd been a senior manager with Google in Singapore. She was female, she was comfortable in the tech world, she had some stellar references. ABC chair Jim Spigelman, I'm told, thought her the answer to his prayers. The board went along. She was certainly a more adventurous and exciting choice than the in-house candidate, the reliable, experienced, safe David Anderson.

But from almost the start there were rumblings of doubt. Mark Scott was a hard act to follow—not because he necessarily made all the right decisions (who does?) but because he was so comfortable in the public realm. Scott could make a speech for any occasion, from farewelling a retiring veteran to taking on the ABC's competitors in wide-ranging surveys of the media landscape. At Senate estimates, when the likes of Tasmanian Senator Eric Abetz bored in with his remorseless attacks on ABC bias, Scott was calm, well-briefed and cogent.

The ABC chair from 2007 to 2012, Maurice Newman is a man of deeply conservative views, and is now one of the ABC's fiercest critics. But I've been told by many sources that Newman and Scott were an impressive double-act, particularly in the corridors of power in Canberra. As one source put it:

'Newman was a wonderful networker, and Scott was a champion schmoozer.'

Scott knew how to talk to his staff, as well as the politicians. 'Mark would almost always call in to the bureau when he was in Canberra,' one of the ABC's gallery reporters told me. 'He'd mention a story you'd done, he'd talk about the latest political issue, ask what you thought. The main thing was, I guess, we felt that he had our back.'

Michelle Guthrie was clearly uncomfortable in this public realm. She made few speeches. Her first Senate estimates hearing became infamous when, having stumbled through an hour and a half's inquisition, she told the senators that if the session didn't end on time she would miss her plane back to Sydney. The committee made sure it ran late. So far as the 'Canberra bubble' is concerned, so derided by our present prime minister, but so crucial to the ABC, she was largely missing in action.

What Guthrie did take seriously was the need to transform the ABC. The digital age beckoned; the age of broadcasting was (prematurely) over. She brought in consultants. She instituted workshops. She commissioned—for the first time ever, I've been told, though I find it hard to believe—a detailed organisational map of the entire corporation, showing precisely who reported to whom, and much else besides.

Since the 2014 budget cut, there had already been hundreds of redundancies. Guthrie pushed through a couple of hundred more. Her primary aim, she said, was to thin down and level off the management structure, saving $50 million that could be put into content creation.

A good slice of this money went to the ABC's forty-eight regional bureaux, many of them tiny. It enabled the creation of eighty new jobs, including video journalists who contribute to state-based television news programs as well as make video for local ABC websites and Facebook pages; the purchase of more capital equipment; and bigger travel budgets. Guthrie is a popular figure in the ABC's far-flung outposts.

But her great idea was the Great Ideas Grant, the GIG. It was a contestable pot of money that anyone in the ABC could pitch for. The aim was to reinvigorate a disillusioned and disengaged staff, and to get fresh new ideas for digital content that would pull in the younger audiences.

To hard-pressed commissioning editors, used to dealing with practised pitches from independent producers whose survival depends on coming up with viable, properly costed program ideas, the GIG was 'an unmitigated disaster'. They found themselves having to assess 'hundreds of half-baked ideas from non-professionals', one of them told me. 'They had no idea how to cost a program, how to make one, how to pitch one. It was run by the Audience and Marketing Division, which had no idea either. We were supposed to "mentor and champion" these people, so we had to spend hours with many of them.'

Only four Great Ideas got a final guernsey in 2017–18. *Unravelled* taps into the apparently inexhaustible audience for 'true crime' investigations. *ABC Life* has been widely panned—especially by commercial media rivals who resent the production by a taxpayer-funded source of material that engages younger audiences in ways that seem made to link to advertisers' messages. It's lively, and clickable, but is it distinctive? Is it the kind of thing the public broadcaster needs to be doing? *Retrofocus* was an idea put up by the ABC's archivists: intriguing little clips from Australia's past, hosted on the News website, and YouTube. And *ABC Kids Listen*, a kids' version of the popular ABC audio app.

All of them focus on digital first. *Unravelled*'s podcasts *Blood on the Tracks* and *Barrenjoey Road* have been accompanied by television programs, which cost far more per hour than the podcasts, and generally rate better, but they're not the point. The point is to reach younger audiences on platforms that they actually use: 'Investing in Audiences', Guthrie labelled her grand vision.

The GIG has not, perhaps, been 'an unmitigated disaster'. But it's not much to show for 200 redundancies, and tens of millions of dollars. Meanwhile, Guthrie's 'transformation' took tangible form in the wholesale reorganisation of the ABC. The Radio and Television content divisions have been done away with. Metropolitan and regional radio stations are now grouped under Local and Regional. So are a hodgepodge of television programs with a sporting or regional flavour—including *Landline*, *Gardening Australia*, *Back Roads* and *Offsiders*. Most television, and much of Radio National, found itself in the Entertainment and Specialist Division. In fact, Radio National—the creative engine of radio, and the pioneer of podcasting in Australia—no longer exists as a distinct entity: it has no overall manager, and no budget of its own. Many of its program-makers feel bereft, and friendless. Only the News Division, which had combined television, radio and online platforms for more than twenty years, was left relatively intact.

The idea was to bring home to ABC content-makers that radio and television are dying technologies: they needed to think more broadly. The work that goes into making a radio or television program has to be refashioned for multiple platforms.

With the reorganisation came workshops, and seminars, and much Google-style jargon. I found, in my wanderings through ABC corridors, that this perpetual 'consultation' caused as much fury and bewilderment as anything that Guthrie did.

One such program of seminars was called 'Leading Transformation'. Busy program executives and editors from all over the country were flown into Sydney and Melbourne once a week for seven weeks to take part in 'learning labs' that lasted all day, led by moderators from an outside consultancy. Booklets were issued, dense with jargon. A sample from *Learning Lab 6*: 'The term "Constructive-Developmental Theory" derives its name from: "developmental", as in cognitive development; "constructive", as in we construct meaning about the world around us; "constructive-developmental", as in the way we construct meaning to develop.'

Participants were led through the Listening Post Method, the 6D Model for Decision-Making, the Immunity Mapping Method: all ways to help team leaders make transformative decisions. But at no stage did this seven-day course discuss the actual decisions to be made, or what 'transformation' it was hoped they would achieve. The people conducting the seminars had no clue about that: they were there to help guide transformation. It wasn't their task to know what was to be transformed into what.

I assume there are industries and companies—perhaps Google is one of them—

where this sort of thing works well. ABC program-makers are sceptics, given to backchat, and irony, and bolshiness. They are professionally inclined to use plain English. And like most people, they respond best to leaders who seem to know where they are going. The consultants found themselves all too often facing open mutiny. The copy of the pamphlet I've acquired has handwritten notes by one participant. Under 'major themes' is written:

> Lack of confidence in leadership
> Too much indecision
> Too much change: 'everything's gonna change next week'
> Frustration
> Dysfunction
> No strategy/vision

The 'Leading Transformation' program would have cost millions. It produced plenty of fury and frustration, but precious little in the way of transformation.

Of course, change is disruptive, by definition. People who have developed skills over years and decades don't always like it when they are told they have to learn new ones. But change leadership is about bringing people with you. Guthrie came across to many of her staff as incurious, and mercurial, and not fully committed. Veteran broadcaster Geraldine Doogue vividly remembers how, in June 2017, at the end of a long day's seminar discussing the ABC's Transformation, Guthrie announced to more than a hundred senior staff: 'Well, I'm off to catch a plane for the Venice Biennale. I'll be there for a week, and I can assure you, I won't be thinking about any of this while I'm there.'

It was supposed to be a throwaway remark. It didn't get a laugh.

And good change management means paying attention to the detail. The details, many felt, weren't looked after. People weren't sure who they were reporting to, or who had the power to make decisions. Managers and commissioning editors found that they no longer had the budgets they thought they would have. Not enough programs had been commissioned, I was told, to fill the schedule in 2019. The obsessive focus was on metrics, the reach of the ABC's digital storytelling.

If change management was failing, it certainly wasn't all Michelle Guthrie's fault. Morale was low in the News Division as well as in Radio National, in Melbourne as well as Sydney. There wasn't much faith in most of the senior managers, whether they were Mark Scott's picks, or Guthrie's.

The only senior manager who seems to enjoy widespread respect is David Anderson, the current acting managing director, the runner-up, so it's said, for the job last time around, and a man who was on the point of leaving a few months before Guthrie's dismissal. But Anderson has been at the ABC for thirty-odd years. He might be a more competent change manager, but he's no disruptor. It remains to be seen if he has a vision of the future he can sell, to the troops or to the politicians.

Meanwhile, by the beginning of 2018, the feud between Guthrie and her chair, Justin

Milne, was deepening. Milne seems to have had one overwhelming obsession: Jetstream. Most people I talked to didn't really understand what it was. A massively souped-up iview, said some, which would allow anyone to access anything the ABC has ever produced, not over the air, but over the internet.

To Milne, it was not a fantasy, but a necessity. He believed the age of broadcasting is drawing to a close: the ABC must equip itself to deliver its services—all its services—through the NBN. Thanks to Jetstream, he argued, the ABC would no longer have to pay the massive costs involved in terrestrial broadcasting of radio and television across a continent. And if the government invested in Jetstream now, it would eventually recoup billions by selling off the digital spectrum the broadcasters no longer needed. (What the commercial broadcasters, who would presumably have to find hundreds of millions of dollars to create their own Jetstreams, would make of Milne's plans he doesn't seem to have discussed.)

Milne's vision seems to have been even larger. 'Imagine, for instance,' he urged his listeners in a speech in July 2018, 'if a single platform could provide all Australians with all the digitised assets of the ABC, and the National Film and Sound Archive, the Australian War Memorial, the National Library of Australia, or state orchestras. This would have significant implications for future education and the digital economy.'[30]

Well, it's certainly a vision. But should that have been the ABC's top priority? It will be a decade, at least, before switching off the ABC's transmitters will be politically feasible. Investing in technology a decade ahead is a perilous endeavour in this era of accelerating change. It is certainly not worth sacrificing the ABC's most precious asset: it's journalistic independence from government. News director Gaven Morris is frank about Jetstream: 'Nobody understood what it meant. Nobody could describe or define what it was meant to be. Now to me … there's a truth that exists, which is that the ABC has to evolve its technology base. There's a debate about the velocity with which you get there … but putting labels and buzzwords around it is less than helpful, so hopefully we will never hear this word Jetstream again.'

Guthrie might have been a tad more enthusiastic. But when in May 2018 the government, without warning, cancelled three years of indexation as an 'efficiency dividend'—yet another one—thus gobbling up most of the precious savings she had made at so much human cost, she clearly gave up. 'If I didn't think that this government was going to provide $500 million for the ABC for modernization [before the budget],' she told *Four Corners*' Sarah Ferguson, 'then after the indexation freeze it became absolutely certain to me that wasn't going to happen.'[31]

Milne still insists that she is wrong. The ABC was planning to apply for an NPP, a New Policy Proposal, which would be funded quite separately from the ABC's ongoing funding. The Bureau of Meteorology and the CSIRO have both had massive digital infrastructure rebuilds, costing hundreds of millions of dollars, funded under the NPP system. Milne says that Fifield and Turnbull had agreed that it was reasonable for the ABC to make a similar bid.

Whether they also hinted that if it wanted its proposal to be taken seriously, the ABC should do something about the likes of Alberici and Probyn, we will probably never know.

And so Guthrie and Milne sailed on to their spectacular collision. Wrong-headed they may both have been, each in their own way. But at least they were wrong about the right question: how to future-proof the ABC, how to equip it to go on serving and reaching the Australian public in ways and on platforms that the public want to use.

An Australian voice

That there's an appetite for what the ABC has to offer can't be doubted. ABC Online is now the second most popular website in the country, after news.com.au—helped, of course, as its rivals will sourly point out, by the fact that it's free. Week after week, *Four Corners*, a program only three years away from its sixtieth birthday, still demonstrates the power of investigative journalism. The royal commission into youth custody in the Northern Territory, the financial services royal commission, the royal commission into aged care, were all directly caused by, or helped along by, *Four Corners* programs. And Sarah Ferguson's investigation into Michelle Guthrie's 'Bitter End' was watched by well over a million Australians as it went to air—and by tens of thousands since.

In the era of fake news, trust is a precious commodity—and the ABC is still trusted, if not as much as it used to be, then far more than any other media organisation, any political party, any bank, or corporation, or institution in the country, other than the High Court and the Federal Reserve.

In November 2000, I spent the best part of a month in Florida, reporting on the aftermath of the presidential election, filming through the windows of a Palm Beach County motel while scrutineers held ballot papers up to the light, trying to determine if a chad were hanging, or intact. When the counting was stopped, by order of the Supreme Court of the United States, George W Bush led Al Gore by the merest handful of votes.

That experience brought home to me how absolutely divided, even back then, the American polity was—and how little trust people had in any institution to be genuinely impartial. The judge who supervised the count in the district where I was filming was dismissed by Republicans as a Democrat. Florida's Secretary of State, Katherine Harris, who oversaw the election statewide, was a strident Republican. The Florida Supreme Court, a majority of whose members were appointed by a Democratic governor, ordered a manual recount. The United States Supreme Court, a majority of whose members were labelled conservative, cancelled the recount.

Every institution in America was predictably partisan, one way or the other.

Today, that mistrust has spread further still—to the FBI, the police forces, the security and intelligence services, the churches, the universities, the scientific consensus, and of course, en masse, to the mainstream media. There is no agreement about what is fake news and what is not, what is true and what is not, what is science and what is faith, what is investigative journalism and what is wild conspiracy theory.

There is no equivalent in the United States of the Australian Electoral Commission, which (with the exception of the egregious Clive Palmer) is trusted by all participants in Australia's elections. No equivalent either of that one-man psephological phenomenon, the ABC's Antony Green, whom I have never heard anyone anywhere accuse of bias. And no American media organisation enjoys a fraction of the trust that poll after poll shows the Australian public still reposes in the ABC.

Undoubtedly, there are some in Australia who see Donald Trump's America as a desirable model for Australia's future. But not many, and I am not one of them. A thriving ABC, that is a part of the lives of most Australians, is one counterweight to the divisiveness of our digitally manipulated polity.

What's needed is simple enough: a chair and directors appointed because they bring to the board essential and relevant expertise—in governance, in media, in Australian culture, in financial acumen—and who understand and support enthusiastically the concept of an independent public broadcaster; a managing director who is able to champion the ABC to the public and the politicians, and set a clear path towards the digital future; funding that is consistent, guaranteed for at least three years, and generous enough to ensure that the ABC can invest in essential digital infrastructure, return some content-making to capitals other than Sydney and Melbourne, and provide some real scrutiny of state affairs; an editorial culture that insists on accuracy, impartiality and programming that reaches out, not just to Australians of all ages, but to Australians of all political views as well; and a political culture in Canberra that accepts what the vast majority of Australians accept—that, like democracy itself, the ABC may not be perfect, but in an age of disintegrating consensus, it is far better than the alternative.

Is that too much to ask?

7.30's chief political correspondent Laura Tingle has been at the ABC for less than a year, after a distinguished career working for News and Fairfax. As we sat and talked in the sunshine outside the ABC's headquarters in Sydney's Ultimo, where she was filling in for Leigh Sales, Tingle became passionate about her role as a senior political reporter for Aunty, in this age of sour contention.

'Because the ABC is under siege,' she said, 'you don't want to do anything that will give people the opportunity to attack it. I feel that very strongly. But caution like that isn't necessarily healthy. People don't understand the point of a public broadcaster as well as they should. They think it's a taxpayer-funded broadcaster, but that's just the means, not the goal, it's not the point of the enterprise.'

'And what is the point?' I asked her.

'The ABC should be the ultimate body that reports without fear or favour, that is beyond the reach of commercial interests, of political interests, and is there to tell stories—not just political stories—but Australian stories, and to reflect an Australian voice.'

I couldn't have put it better myself.

Notes

1 *7.30*, ABC TV, 27 September 2018, https://www.abc.net.au/7.30/justin-milne-resigns-as-abc-chairman/10314302
2 KS Inglis, *Whose ABC?*, Black Inc., Melbourne, 2006, p. 228.
3 Jonathan Holmes, 'The Media War', in I Bickerton and M Pearson (eds), *43 Days: The Gulf War*, Text Publishing and ABC Books, Sydney, 1991, p. 199.
4 Geraldine Doogue, 'Power, Vulnerability and Scapegoats', in *Griffith Review*, no. 1, Spring 2003, https://griffithreview.com/articles/power-vulnerability-and-scapegoats/. For comments by David Hill and Peter Manning, see 'Correspondence', in *Griffith Review*, no. 2, Summer 2003–04 (not available online).
5 Janet Albrechtsen, 'Fan-girl Ferguson Would Be a Poor Fit to Chair the ABC', *The Australian*, 2 October 2018, https://www.theaustralian.com.au/opinion/columnists/janet-albrechtsen/fangirl-ferguson-would-be-a-poor-fit-to-chair-abc/news-story/3e4f59d58784f92ea2567dcc02a28897

NOTES

6 Australian Government, Senate Environment and Communications References Committee Inquiry into Allegations of Political Interference in the ABC, public hearing, 30 November 2018, Hansard transcript, p. 6, https://parlinfo.aph.gov.au/parlInfo/download/committees/commsen/0c022f36-fab2-4c0b-8570-052704b388f2/toc_pdf/Environment%20and%20Communications%20References%20Committee_2018_11_30_6819.pdf;fileType=application%2Fpdf#search=%22committees/commsen/0c022f36-fab2-4c0b-8570-052704b388f2/0000%22

7 Australian Government, Department of Communications and the Arts, Inquiry into the Competitive Neutrality of the National Broadcasters, Fairfax Media Response to Issues Paper, 22 June 2018, https://www.communications.gov.au/sites/default/files/submissions/fairfax_media_-_25_june_2018.pdf

8 Inquiry into the Competitive Neutrality of the National Broadcasters, Report of the Expert Panel, 12 December 2018, https://www.communications.gov.au/documents/inquiry-competitive-neutrality-national-broadcasters-report-expert-panel

9 Australian Government, Parliamentary Library, Bills Digest no. 2, 2018–19, http://apo.org.au/system/files/182121/apo-nid182121-958571.pdf

NOTES

10 Inglis, pp. 545–50.
11 ibid., pp. 549–50.
12 Senate Environment and Communications References Committee Inquiry into Allegations of Political Interference in the ABC, submission no. 12, 27 November 2018, pp. 4–5, https://www.aph.gov.au/Parliamentary_Business/Committees/Senate/Environment_and_Communications/ABCInterferenceAllegations/Submissions
13 ABC Editorial Guidance Note: 'Differentiating between Factual Reporting, Analysis and Opinion', July 2014, https://edpols.abc.net.au/guidance/differentiating-between-factual-reporting-analysis-and-opinion/
14 'Bitter End', *Four Corners*, ABC TV, 12 November 2018, https://www.abc.net.au/4corners/bitter-end/10490434
15 Senate Environment and Communications References Committee Inquiry into Allegations of Political Interference in the ABC, Hansard transcript, pp. 11–12.
16 'Bitter End'.
17 ibid.
18 Senate Environment and Communications References Committee Inquiry into Allegations of Political Interference in the ABC, Hansard transcript, pp. 28–9.

NOTES

19 Australian Communications and Media Authority investigation BI-347, 5 April 2018, https://www.acma.gov.au/theACMA/2018-television-investigations

20 *Media Watch*, ABC TV, 7 May 2018, https://www.abc.net.au/mediawatch/episodes/media-regulator-slaps-abc/9972246

21 Laura Tingle, '"You've Got to Play to the Base": Why the ABC is a Political Football', ABC News Online, 9 June 2018, https://www.abc.net.au/news/2018-06-09/laura-tingle-why-the-abc-is-a-political-football/9850360

22 *Insiders*, ABC TV, 30 September 2018, at 38 min 46 secs, https://www.abc.net.au/insiders/sunday-30-september-full-program/10322604

23 Paul Kelly, 'We Need the ABC—It's Time It Realised that It Needs Us', *The Weekend Australian*, 3 October 2018, https://www.theaustralian.com.au/opinion/columnists/paul-kelly/we-need-the-abc-its-time-it-realised-that-it-needs-us/news-story/097f5c019e3de6b0b362ffe92359fa04

24 ibid.

25 See for example Jay Rosen, 'The View from Nowhere: Questions and Answers', *PressThink* blog, 10 November 2010, http://pressthink.org/2010/11/the-view-from-nowhere-questions-and-answers/

NOTES

26 Bill Keller, 'Is Glenn Greenwald the Future of News?', *The New York Times*, 27 October 2013, https://www.nytimes.com/2013/10/28/opinion/a-conversation-in-lieu-of-a-column.html?_r=0

27 Katharine Murphy, *On Disruption*, Melbourne University Press, Melbourne, 2018, p. 98.

28 Quentin Dempster, *Death Struggle*, Allen & Unwin, Sydney, 2000, p. 76.

29 *7.30*, ABC TV, 27 September 2018.

30 Justin Milne, 'An ABC Fit for the Future', speech to the American Chamber of Commerce, Sydney, 11 July 2018, http://about.abc.net.au/speeches/an-abc-fit-for-the-future/

31 'Bitter End'.

Acknowledgements

I interviewed some thirty people while researching this little book—among them David Anderson, Bruce Belsham, Lucy Carter, Barrie Cassidy, Geraldine Doogue, Ticky Fullerton, David Hill, Peter Manning, Peter McEvoy, Michael Mason, Jim Middleton, Gaven Morris, Kim Porteous, Andrew Probyn, Norman Swan, Laura Tingle, Chris Uhlmann and Ollie Wards. The others would, I think, not thank me for naming them, but they know who they are. Quentin Dempster, Sarah Ferguson, Sally Neighbour, Matt Peacock and Deb Richards helped in other ways. My thanks to all of them.

ACKNOWLEDGEMENTS

At MUP, Louise Adler was persistent, Sally Heath encouraging, Louise Stirling and Eugenie Baulch meticulous.

It's your ABC, but everyone has their own Aunty. Mine has given me a career that has been full of interest, creative reward and stimulating colleagues too numerous by far to name. One, Shaun Hoyt, was a workmate, off and on, for a decade, and has been my partner for twenty more. Supporting a grouchy writer, she's discovered, is even harder than putting up with a stressed television reporter. But she did, as she always has.